I AM

Name:

Strong

Copyright © 2021 Newbee Publication

ALL RIGHTS RESERVED

Thanks for Purchase

Scan QR code for more publications

This book may not be reproduced or transmitted in any form or by any means, electronic or mechanical, without written permission from the author.

I have done this before, and I can do it again.

I have done this before, and I can do it again.

I have done this before, and I can do it again.

Breathing Exercise

Put your finger on number 1 and start breathing in a while, moving your finger to 6, holding your breath for 7 & 8 and starting Breathing out to 9 while moving down your finger to 15.

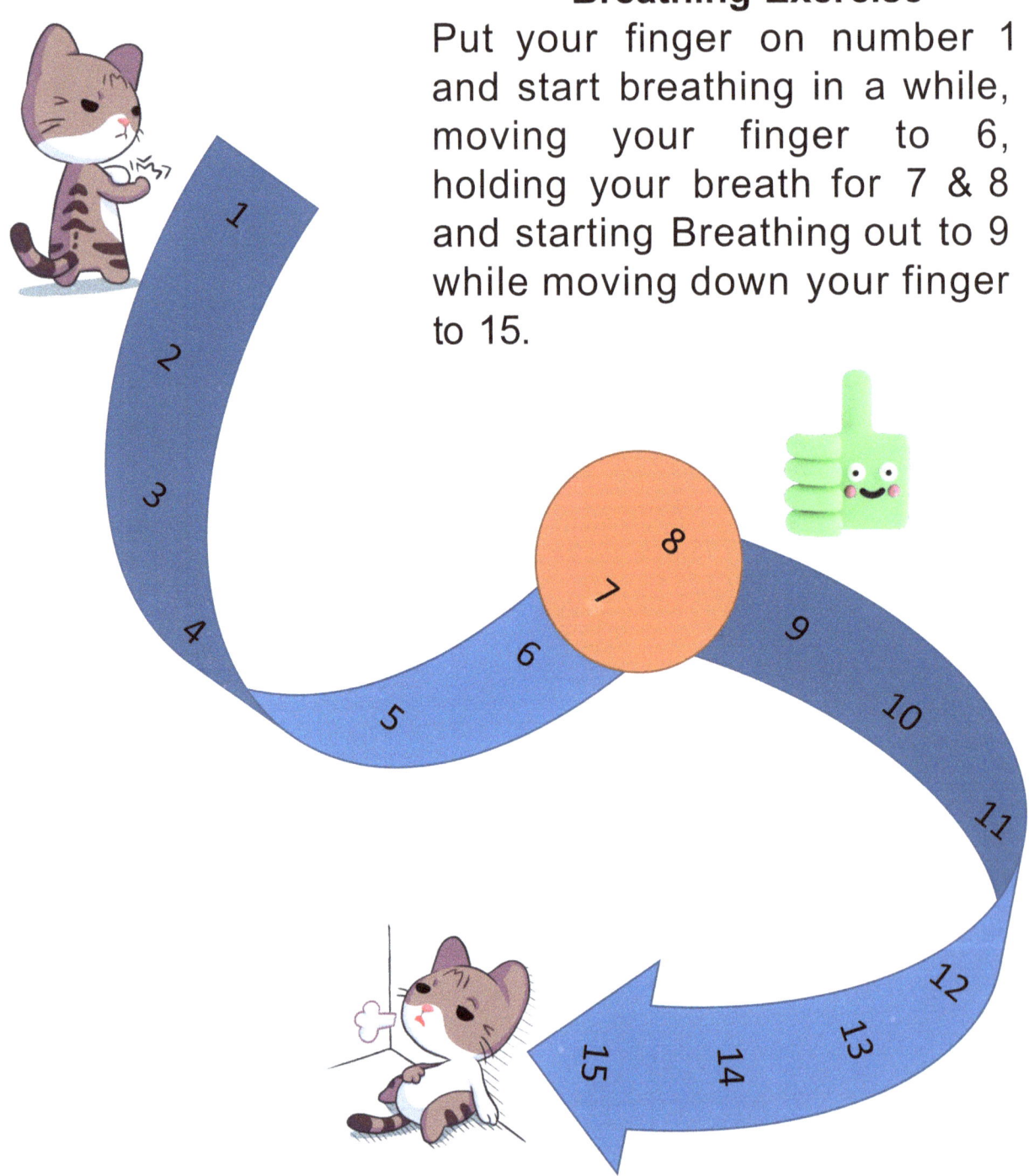

Circle any of the things below that make you anxious:

- School or going to school
- Tests and exams in school
- In front of others
- Meeting new people
- Your body
- Your sexuality
- Your safety
- Class presentations
- Homework
- A particular class
- Your report card
- Asking for something from someone
- Talking with your parents about your problems
- What your future holds
- Your parents' marriage
- Your family life
- Talking with other kids
- Violence or war
- Money or job in future
- What do you look like
- Whether people like you or not
- Your siblings
- Religion
- Illness
- Your athletic skills

Whenever negative thoughts pop-ups, stop them and write affirmations given in this book & repeat them in your head.

I take things one day at a time.

I take things one day at a time.

I take things one day at a time.

I take things one day at a time.

Write things below that make you feel happy and relaxed:

- _____
- _____
- _____
- _____
- _____
- _____
- _____
- _____
- _____
- _____

I have everything I need for a happy life.
I have everything I need for a happy life.
I have everything I need for a happy life.

I have everything I need for a happy life.

I am becoming a better version of myself.

I am becoming a better version of myself.

I am becoming a better version of myself.

Difficulties come and go, and this too shall pass.

Difficulties come and go, and this too shall pass.

Difficulties come and go, and this too shall pass.

Difficulties come and go, and this

Colour the circles in Red, Yellow, Green and Blue

I am improving every day in every way.

I am improving every day in every way.

I am improving every day in every way.

I am capable of solving my problem
that I face.

I am capable of solving my problem
that I face.

I am capable of solving my problem
that I face.

The feelings of panic are leaving my body.

The feelings of panic are leaving my body.

The feelings of panic are leaving my body.

I can overcome my anxieties.

I can overcome my anxieties.

I can overcome my anxieties.

I can overcome my anxieties.

Breathing exercise

Put your finger on number 1 and start breathing in a while, moving your finger to 6 and hold your breath to 7 & 8 and start Breath out to 9 while moving down your finger to 1. hold your breath for 7 & 8, start breathing in again after reaching to 1; keep following for 5 times.

I am free of anything that weighs me down.

I am free of anything that weighs me down.

I am free of anything that weighs me down.

I am free of anything that weighs me down.

I am freeing myself from the stress.

I am freeing myself from the stress.

I am freeing myself from the stress.

I am freeing myself from the stress.

I am freeing myself from the stress.

I am relaxing each part of my body.

I am relaxing each part of my body.

I am relaxing each part of my body.

I am relaxing each part of my body.

Colour the double bubbles in rainbow colours

My body is calm.

My body is calm.

My body is calm.

My body is calm.

I will get through today.

I will get through today.

I will get through today.

I will get through today.

I will get through today.

I welcome a sense of calm into my life.

I welcome a sense of calm into my life.

I welcome a sense of calm into my life.

I welcome a sense of calm into my life.

I welcome a sense of calm into my life.

Breathing exercise

Put your finger on number 1 and start breathing in a while, moving your finger to 6 and hold your breath to 7 & 8 and start Breath out to 9 while moving down your finger to 1. hold your breath for 7 & 8, start breathing in again after reaching to 1; keep following for 5 times.

All is well in my world.

All is well in my world.

All is well in my world.

All is well in my world.

All is well in my world.

I allow myself to feel this way without any judgment.

I allow myself to feel this way without any judgment.

I allow myself to feel this way without any judgment.

I open my soul to peace.

I open my soul to peace.

I open my soul to peace.

I open my soul to peace.

Everything will be fine, and it's okay.

Everything will be fine, and it's okay.

Everything will be fine, and it's okay.

Everything will be fine, and it's okay.

Everything will be fine, and it's okay.

Everything will be fine, and it's okay.

Colour this Mandala whatever colour you like

I am brave, and I can do it.

I am brave, and I can do it.

I am brave, and I can do it.

I am brave, and I can do it.

I am brave, and I can do it.

I am brave, and I can do it.

I am relaxed, calm and collected.

I am relaxed, calm and collected.

I am relaxed, calm and collected.

I am relaxed, calm and collected.

I am relaxed, calm and collected.

I am in control of my day.

I am in control of my day.

I am in control of my day.

I am in control of my day.

I am trying my best, and that is enough.

I am trying my best, and that is enough.

I am trying my best, and that is enough.

Draw clouds, birds, trees and a river

I can surmount any and all situations.

I can surmount any and all situations.

I can surmount any and all situations.

I can surmount any and all situations.

I am here, and everything is fine.

I am here, and everything is fine.

I am here, and everything is fine.

I am here, and everything is fine.

I am breathing slowly and feeling
relaxed.
I am breathing slowly and feeling
relaxed.
I am breathing slowly and feeling
relaxed.
I am breathing slowly and feeling
relaxed.
I am breathing slowly and feeling
relaxed.

It's all right, and all is well.

It's all right, and all is well.

It's all right, and all is well.

It's all right, and all is well.

It's all right, and all is well.

Draw multicolour lines in between these

Life is straightforward and interesting.

Life is straightforward and interesting.

Life is straightforward and interesting.

Life is straightforward and interesting.

Life is straightforward and interesting.

The air I am breathing in is making
me feel calmer.
The air I am breathing in is making
me feel calmer.
The air I am breathing in is making
me feel calmer.

The air I am breathing in is making
me feel calmer.

I am now in control.

I am now in control.

I am now in control.

I am now in control.

I am now in control.

Everything is under my control.

Everything is under my control.

Everything is under my control.

Everything is under my control.

Everything is under my control.

Everything is under my control.

I am strong & can overcome any obstacle.

I am strong & can overcome any obstacle.

I am strong & can overcome any obstacle.

I am strong & can overcome any obstacle.

I got this and can do it.

I got this and can do it.

I got this and can do it.

I got this and can do it.

I got this and can do it.

Colour this Mandala whatever colour you like, and draw longer Petals

It is okay if I do not feel okay all
the time.

It is okay if I do not feel okay all
the time.

It is okay if I do not feel okay all
the time.

It is okay if I do not feel okay all
the time.

I am loved and supported by my parents.

I am loved and supported by my parents.

I am loved and supported by my parents.

I am loved and supported by my parents.

I can feel the shift towards peace.

I can feel the shift towards peace.

I can feel the shift towards peace.

I can feel the shift towards peace.

I know I am worthy of peace.

I know I am worthy of peace.

I know I am worthy of peace.

I know I am worthy of peace.

The peace that I need is inside me.

The peace that I need is inside me.

The peace that I need is inside me.

Draw what you see in these squiggly lines

Nobody can help me achieve peace but me.

Nobody can help me achieve peace but me.

Nobody can help me achieve peace but me.

Nobody can help me achieve peace but me.

The power is in my hands.

The power is in my hands.

The power is in my hands.

The power is in my hands.

The power is in my hands.

I know the problems are temporary.

I know the problems are temporary.

I know the problems are temporary.

I know the problems are temporary.

I know the problems are temporary.

I am capable of handling anything.

I am capable of handling anything.

I am capable of handling anything.

I am capable of handling anything.

I am capable of handling anything.

All problems have solutions.

All problems have solutions.

All problems have solutions.

All problems have solutions.

I feel relaxed when I breathe slowly and feel my breath.

I feel relaxed when I breathe slowly and feel my breath.

I feel relaxed when I breathe slowly and feel my breath.

I feel relaxed when I breathe slowly and feel my breath.

Colour this Mandala whatever colour you like

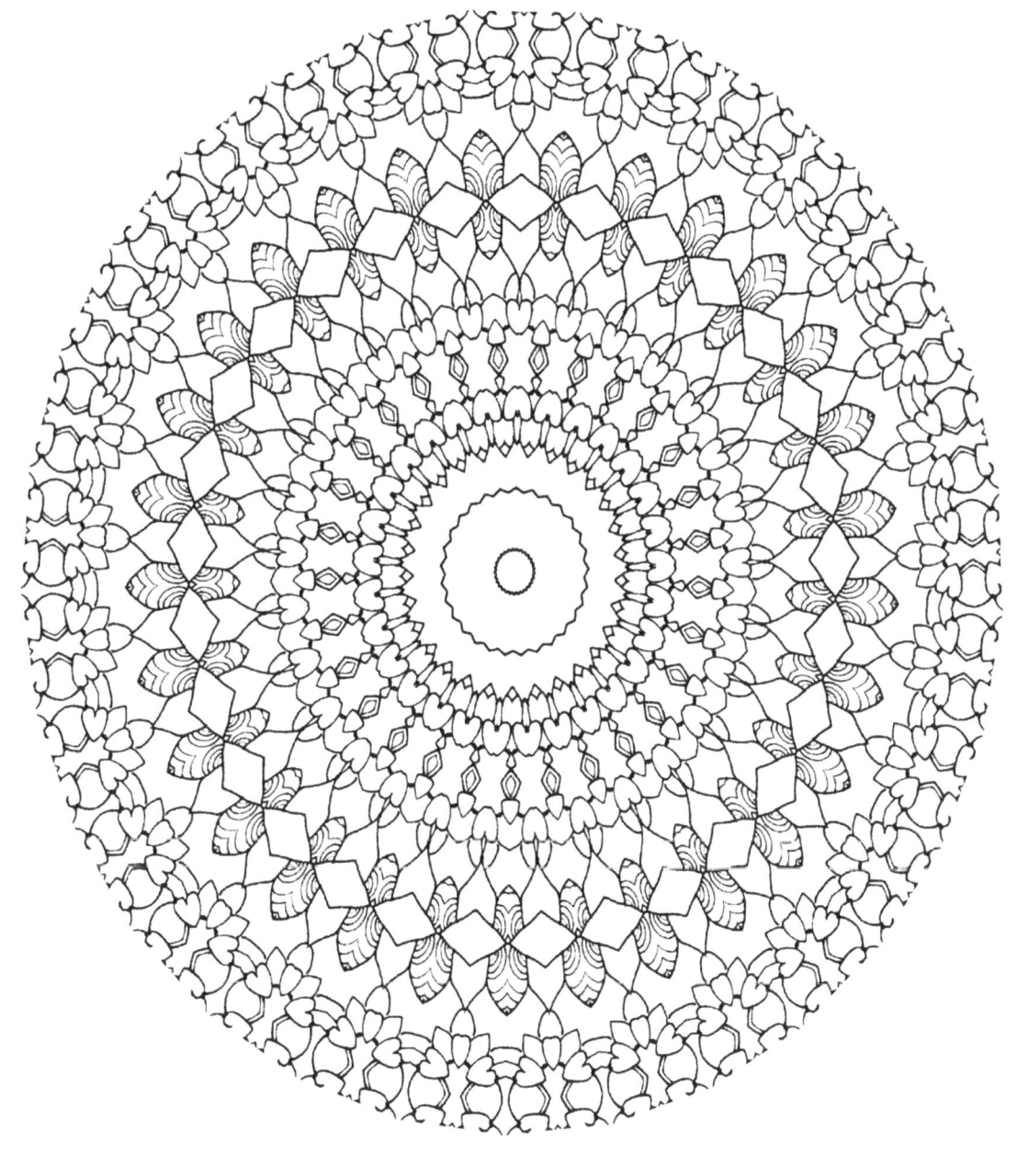

I welcome the feeling of calm.

I welcome the feeling of calm.

I welcome the feeling of calm.

I welcome the feeling of calm.

I welcome the feeling of calm.

I feel light and free from worries.

I feel light and free from worries.

I feel light and free from worries.

I feel light and free from worries.

Nothing can disrupt my peace.

Nothing can disrupt my peace.

Nothing can disrupt my peace.

Nothing can disrupt my peace.

I strive to achieve inner peace.

I strive to achieve inner peace.

I strive to achieve inner peace.

I strive to achieve inner peace.

Breathing exercise

Put your finger on number 1 and start breathing in a while, moving your finger to 6 and hold your breath to 7 & 8 and start Breath out to 9 while moving down your finger to 1. hold your breath for 7 & 8, start breathing in again after reaching to 1; keep following for 5 times.

My life is always at peace.

My life is always at peace.

My life is always at peace.

My life is always at peace.

My life is always at peace.

Harmony and peace surround me.

Harmony and peace surround me.

Harmony and peace surround me.

Harmony and peace surround me.

I can be relaxed in all situations.

I can be relaxed in all situations.

I can be relaxed in all situations.

I can be relaxed in all situations.

I can be relaxed in all situations.

I am surrounded by positive energy.

I am surrounded by positive energy.

I am surrounded by positive energy.

I am surrounded by positive energy.

I am surrounded by positive energy.

I am letting peace into my body with every breath.

I am letting peace into my body with every breath.

I am letting peace into my body with every breath.

I am letting peace into my body with every breath.

I am letting peace into my body with every breath.

I can feel the connection to my inner peace.

I can feel the connection to my inner peace.

I can feel the connection to my inner peace.

I can feel the connection to my inner peace.

Draw coloured circles in this Mandala as many as you like

I am grateful for the peace I have right now.

I am grateful for the peace I have right now.

I am grateful for the peace I have right now.

I am grateful for the peace I have right now.

I give myself permission to remove
stress from my life.

I give myself permission to remove
stress from my life.

I give myself permission to remove
stress from my life.

I take my peace with me wherever I go.

I take my peace with me wherever I go.

I take my peace with me wherever I go.

I take my peace with me wherever I go.

I take my peace with me wherever I go.

I feel deeply calm and relaxed.

I feel deeply calm and relaxed.

I feel deeply calm and relaxed.

I feel deeply calm and relaxed.

Every cell in my body has a
positive vibration.
Every cell in my body has a
positive vibration.
Every cell in my body has a
positive vibration

Every cell in my body has a
positive vibration.

Colour this Mandala whatever colour you like

I attract peace and calm people into my life.

I attract peace and calm people into my life.

I attract peace and calm people into my life.

I attract peace and calm people into my life.

I am getting better and better in all
my ways.
I am getting better and better in all
my ways.

I am getting better and better in all
my ways.

It's Okay to be scared, but I know
how to control my thoughts.
It's Okay to be scared, but I know
how to control my thoughts.

It's Okay to be scared, but I know
how to control my thoughts.

I know how to control my thoughts.
I know how to control my thoughts.
I know how to control my thoughts.
I know how to control my thoughts.

I welcome calm in my life.

Difficulties can come and shall pass.

I am leading a happy life.

I am going away from stressors.

I am not feeling panic about small things.

Breathing exercise

Put your finger on number 1 and start breathing in a while, moving your finger to 6 and hold your breath to 7 & 8 and start Breath out to 9 while moving down your finger to 1. hold your breath for 7 & 8, start breathing in again after reaching to 1; keep following for 5 times.

I am getting better and better physically and mentally.

- My life is simple and Good.

My challenges are opportunities to learn new skills.

I choose to be kind to myself.

Every day in every way, I get better and better.

I accomplish everything I set my mind to.

I have the power to create my happiness.

I am learning valuable lessons from myself every day.

I put my energy into things that matter to me.

I am grateful for another day to make a positive contribution.

I give myself the care and attention that I deserve.

Every day is a constant state of learning.

I am practising loving my life.

I am not afraid of being wrong.

My life is meaningful and essential.

I am open to things working out for me.

I will go easy on myself whatever I do today.

I over analyse the situation; I need to be calm.

Every moment is a chance for a new beginning.

I trust myself, but I don't believe everything that other thinks.

I am in control, so what could possibly go wrong?

I don't worry about what others think of me.

I take deep breaths when I feel anxious.

I am allowing myself to slow down.

Everyone makes mistakes, so what if I made a mistake?

I will try my best today; I know I am good at trying.

I trust myself, and I always make good choices.

We would appreciate it if you could give a review on google
For More Publications visit our website

www.newbeepublication.com

www.ingramcontent.com/pod-product-compliance
Lightning Source LLC
Chambersburg PA
CBHW051331110526
44590CB00032B/4483